On Getting to the Point

On Getting to the Point

Dave Yewman

DASH Consulting, Inc.
Vancouver, Washington

DASH Consulting, Inc.
2712 NW 142nd Circle
Vancouver, WA 98685
www.dashconsultinginc.com

11 10 09 08 07   1 2 3 4 5
ISBN: 978-0-615-17058-9
Library of Congress Control Number: 2007939477

Design by Jennifer Omner, ALL Publications

Contents

Introduction

There is a staggering amount of bullshit flying around when it comes to communications.

It's sad. But not really that surprising.

It's also easy to fix. If we care to take the time.

What you hold in your hand is a collection of essays—rants really—on everything from cell phone etiquette to a porn star's public speaking angst; from senior executives who can't answer simple questions to hideously-written press releases; from the dreaded "Death by PowerPoint" syndrome to politicians who simply don't know when to shut up.

Sometimes the rants include easy fixes to common mistakes; sometimes they're just rants.

Over the past several years, I wrote something when

I felt compelled and then posted an essay to my Web site, www.dashconsultinginc.com.

I called the newsletter, the *Communications Grok*, and my wife shook her head and said, "What the hell is a Grok?"

Well (honey), it's a term I stole from a 1961 science fiction novel called *Stranger in a Strange Land*, by Robert Heinlein. To "grok" something means to thoroughly understand it, to "get" it. During the Internet bubble of the late 1990s, there was a newsletter called the *Media Grok*, and I was particularly fond of it. Alas, it didn't survive the bubble's burst, but the idea stuck with me.

As someone famous once said, "The biggest misconception about communication is that it ever took place." That's the truly sad thing about all this noise that substitutes for real communications—it wastes precious time and real money when people don't realize the difference between saying something and just moving their lips.

So when it comes to bullshit, how do we handle a world that's full of it? Here are a few thoughts on what my thirteen-year-old might call, "How to deal . . ."

Dave Yewman

Vancouver, Washington

September 27, 2007

1
It's Hard

Tyla Wynn is a porn star. On January 8 she won an award for "excellence in a multi-person scene" at an adult film industry convention in Las Vegas for *Too Hot to Handle*, one of one hundred and fifty movies she made in 2005 in which she presumably did all manner of things with all manner of folks while wearing little or no clothing.

But when it came to accepting the award on stage (fully clothed) before three thousand people, Wynn was clearly nervous. "Speaking in front of people is hard," she told a reporter. I'll avoid the obvious pun here but suffice to say it's not easy even for, ahem, professional performers to speak before crowds of people.

Wynn isn't alone. Rapper-turned-business-executive Jay-Z had to give a presentation to a group of recording industry executives last summer. "When you're on stage it's like, 'What's up Cleveland? Wave your hands in the air, say ho,'" he told a reporter afterward. "But to stand in front of people and give a speech and talk about the things you're trying to do, it's not easy."

No, it's not, but as Jay-Z steers his billion-dollar record label and ponders taking the helm of Island/Def Jam Records, he's going to be giving a lot of speeches.

I've coached hundreds of business executives—and the occasional celebrity—in the past several years, and it's safe to say that people at all levels of the corporate and entertainment worlds have the same fears and often make the same mistakes when speaking publicly.

The good news is that there's an easy cure, and it involves two things many people possess: commitment and a video camera.

If you want to give a fabulous speech, you have to practice early and practice often. Some people can wing it and succeed, but chances are you will have to work at it, and video-taping your practice sessions does two valuable things.

1. Videotaping lets you see yourself as others see you—an often humbling experience that sanity-checks both messages and messenger. It can be extremely tough to watch. But there's nothing like it for making your speech better.

2. Videotaping is also a terrific note taker that allows you to capture stories, analogies, and examples, and arrange them in a logical flow. We're all better speakers when we're telling stories.

It's perfectly natural for you to prefer crawling across a bed of nails rather than watching yourself on tape. Get over it. Because ultimately it's arrogant to think that video can make everyone better except you. It's not complicated, but as rappers, actors, and porn stars well know, some things in life are just hard.

2
Bored Presentations

We've all been there: a darkened conference room, a boring speaker, a lengthy slide deck. No amount of coffee can stimulate our interest. We think dark thoughts about the presenter, and if there was a gong in the corner of the room, we'd line up to bang it and end the drudgery.

I once knew a technical evangelist at a major software company who was excited to have "trimmed" his presentation down to forty-five slides. Problem was he only had twenty minutes to deliver his message. Disaster doesn't even begin to describe what happened.

The evangelist isn't alone. Many business executives have a frightening inability to get to the point—some of them could bore for America. And that's a damn shame because they probably have something useful to say. Combining bad slides with a boring delivery kills communications quicker than you can say, "George W. Bush."

Never has such an important skill been so widely neglected. Surveys consistently show communications is the most important factor in being a successful executive. And in the next few years, everyone will get their fifteen minutes of fame; communications will be increasingly instant and continually compressed into bite-sized chunks for our consumption—think CNN on your cell phone or ESPN on your Palm Pilot. It might not be effective communications, but it will be ubiquitous.

But as technology enables broader communications, the potential for ineffective presentations also increases. So on behalf of bored audiences everywhere, here are two suggestions to help everyone communicate more clearly: Rule 3:12 and Rule 5:2.

Rule 3:12 (three bullets, twelve words per slide)
While it's a useful product, Microsoft PowerPoint has become a crutch for crappy presenters. In many presentations

there is simply too much information crammed onto each slide and too many slides by far—leading to the dreaded "Death by PowerPoint" syndrome for which there is no known cure. But chances are everyone in your audience can read. So keep the bullets short. You talk. The slides support your key points.

How does that look? Instead of a bullet that reads "Company experienced 2002 net revenue growth of 34 percent in Asia/Pacific, 25 percent in Europe, 14 percent in North America" the bullet is, simply, "Growth" or "34, 25, 14" or, better yet, a world map with the numbers superimposed. And if you combine a clear slide with a compelling delivery and an engaging anecdote on why growth in Asia was so high, you'll get the point across.

For a thirty-minute presentation ten to twelve slides is plenty. The gory details can be put online or on handouts. The benefit to such brevity includes an engaged audience and clearly communicated messages—and, after all, isn't that the point? Encyclopedic knowledge of a subject is impressive, but no one likes having an encyclopedia put on slides and read to them. But even kicking away the PowerPoint crutch doesn't result in a fabulous presentation. For that, we need humans. And that's where the second rule comes in.

Rule 5:2 (five out-loud rehearsals, two on tape)
Any audience judges any presenter on the first thirty to sixty seconds of a speech or presentation—a mental "So what? Who cares?" test that we all apply. That thirty-minute speech should be rehearsed out loud five times, and two of those rehearsals should be taped. Most people have a strong aversion to seeing themselves on videotape, but it's the absolute best way to hone delivery of a presentation. As one of my clients once put it, "Videotaping is ugly, but it works."

And that's no surprise. Did you ever wonder why actors deliver their lines with such panache and passion? You think they roll out of their trailers and just wing it when the director yells "Action!"? No, they rehearse—and you should, too. If video is simply too daunting or impractical, use a microcassette tape recorder to capture your presentation as you drive to work.

One useful—and private—trick is to use the bathroom. With your slides and speaker notes close by, talk to that person in the mirror, notice his gestures, check out her pauses and cadence, listen for his "ums" and "ahs," observe her posture. It's free, private, and it's somewhere most of us already visit at least a few times each day. Once you've mastered the bathroom delivery, tape your presentation and review it. If you can stand it, have a trusted friend or colleague critique your performance.

Your presentation is so much more than words. In fact, studies show that up to ninety-three percent of speaking impact is nonverbal; so while you may feel like a dork rehearsing in the bathroom mirror, and hate seeing yourself on videotape, it can pay off in a major way come presentation time.

Ultimately, effective communications is up to you—and other business executives. It takes preparation—combined with a judicious, restrained use of PowerPoint—to avoid snoozing audiences. Following a few simple rules can't hurt, either.

3
PowerPoint Makes You Stupid

June 2006

I call it *the blob.*

You have to deliver a presentation. *Not to worry,* you think, *I'll just use Bill's slide deck and add a few slides from Suzy's board presentation, then combine them with that sales meeting PowerPoint I did.*

Bad move.

You've just taken the easy way out and cobbled together a blob: an often-meaningless compendium of slideware that lacks a clear point. It's really tough to effectively communicate the blob. It's like trying to look good by assembling a wardrobe of borrowed clothes—an unlikely route to success.

As a presentation coach, I see a lot of blobs: untidy jumbles of bullet points and mismatched graphics that ramble and bore audiences stiff; Save-As masterpieces culled from slide decks that litter the corporate computer network. The most painful part of the blob? Watching otherwise smart, capable people try to deliver it.

The good news? There is an easy way to avoid the blob and make sure you effectively deliver a message to your audience. The bad news? It's what George W. Bush might call "hard work."

But as a bonus you'll actually get your message across.

Try this: a week or so before your presentation, block some time on your calendar and go somewhere quiet—a conference room, a spare office, your den, Starbucks—it doesn't matter. But shut off all your electronic leashes and just think for a while.

Take a stack of sticky notes. Think about your audience and the key points you want them to understand after you have finished talking. Think about how much time you will have and what stories and examples you can use to illustrate what you want to say. Write two or three words describing each idea on the sticky notes.

If you spend forty-five minutes in think mode, you should have dozens of sticky notes spread out on a table. Now organize them into buckets. It doesn't have to be precise. Just group the notes by general topic.

Next, rank those groups by order of importance. Have you duplicated anything? Is there a clear message emerging? Can you think of a logical flow that connects the groups?

If so, congratulations; you've built a presentation that just might make sense. If not, call in the cavalry. Get some help from trusted peers or colleagues, and listen to their input. Or imagine the presentation before yours runs long and the time for your presentation is cut in half. What would you say? That's the nutshell of your presentation.

After the tableful of sticky notes points you in a clear direction, then—and only then—start thinking about PowerPoint slides. The slides are a visual aid—not an entire presentation. Want to talk about your company's contract with General Motors? Don't put the details up on the screen, just put the GM logo or a photo of its nearby plant, and then talk through the details. If you write it, they will read it—instead of listening to you.

After constructing your presentation's flow, carefully picking slides and thinking through what you want the audience to take away, it's time to rehearse—out loud and at least four to five times.

I know what you're thinking—*who has this kind of time?* Well, respectfully: you do. We all do. You have fifteen minutes a day to become a better presenter—you shower, you jog, you drive to work. Use that time to carve out a few minutes and practice out loud. If Apple boss Steve Jobs spends four to five hours rehearsing his hour-long keynote presentations, you can find some time. Your audience will thank you for it.

But most importantly, as you develop messages, prepare slides, and rehearse for that big presentation, avoid taking the easy way out; avoid the blob.

4
Ten Tips for Talking Heads

July 2003

Andy Warhol once said that everyone will be world-famous for fifteen minutes. So when that time comes, don't screw it up. Follow these ten tips for broadcast success, whether you're talking to Matt and Katie via satellite uplink or your employees via a Webcast.

1. Eye contact is king—if you're on set, focus on your interviewer and NEVER look at the camera. However, if you're on a satellite hookup maintain eye contact with the camera lens at all times. When pausing to think, look down—not up—so viewers won't think you're rolling your eyes.

2. Dress for success—dress conservatively. Wear solid colors—blues, browns—no plaid, no checkered patterns. And no white shirts. It's a good idea to have a backup outfit on hand in case of coffee spills or rising levels of perspiration (TV lights can be extremely hot). Don't wear a hat or anything that would cast a shadow on your face. Men: hair combed neatly, clean-shaven. Women: hair pulled back off face (if it's long), light makeup. If possible wear contacts rather than glasses (TV lights can reflect off the glass).

3. Strike a pose—posture matters; if you're on set, you'll want to lean forward around twenty degrees when you talk—it'll open up your diaphragm, which increases your air supply. It prevents you from slumping, plus you'll look engaged in the discussion. A good rule of thumb is not to let your back touch the back of your chair. Sit with your feet flat on the floor, shoulders square, and your butt firmly in the back of the chair.

4. House of pancake—no one wants to look like Nixon in the 1960 debates—a layer of pancake makeup will prevent the glistening that hot TV lights can produce. Guys usually cringe at the thought of makeup but, hey, if it's good enough for the leader of the free world, it's good enough for them.

5. Acknowledge and bridge—you have "must air" points or key messages prepared—use them. Attention spans are short. Your on-air time is also short. Acknowledge and answer any questions you're asked but always try to bridge back to those key messages during your interview. Also, reiterate those messages if you're asked to provide a sound check or give a summation/closing thought.

6. Practice makes perfect—being on TV under lights, wearing makeup, and looking into a camera is an artificial environment and can be extremely stressful. You literally have seconds to sell your story. Practice in your bathroom mirror with a stopwatch—or if you can stand it, use a video camera and have a trusted friend/family member/colleague critique your delivery. This sort of preparation will enable you to exude calm cool confidence during the actual interview. It also prevents a case of the "ums"—a disease that causes a lack of future TV appearances.

7. Remove distractions—turn cell phones and pagers off, lose the gum, remove coins from pockets, and don't hold a pen unless you're Bob Dole or disciplined enough not to play with it on camera. If you're on a satellite hookup, ask the technician to turn off the TV set by the camera so you're not tempted to look down and see how you look during the interview. Request that you be outfitted with an earpiece and a lavalier microphone before going on-air to make sure it fits/works and is comfortable. Also, avoid chairs that swivel and rock—they're simply too tempting, especially when you get nervous.

8. Energy matters—everything counts on TV—posture, energy, facial expression. For proof just watch the delivery of TV news anchors. Smile, you're not under deposition! This can be fun. If possible, exercise before going on camera so your blood is flowing and you're fully awake (a little caffeine might also help). This will help avoid what one CEO called "Dead Man Talking" syndrome.

9. Tell stories—media outlets tell stories for a living. Help them do their job and it will benefit you and your company. Examples, anecdotes, and graphics can all help communicate your message. Use them. Telling stories also helps break your conversation into sound bites—the lingua franca of TV.

10. Expect the unexpected—TV news is dynamic— an in-studio interview can quickly change to a satellite hookup; what was to be taped can suddenly be carried live;

reporters will sometimes try to ambush you. Remain calm, be prepared, and try to accommodate any unexpected changes.

Finally, someone once asked Dan Rather what he'd learned in thirty-plus years of broadcasting. He replied, "Don't eat spinach before you go on the air." Good advice. During those fifteen minutes of fame, no one wants to be remembered as the person with a green glob on his teeth.

5
We Can Hear You Now

June 2004

It was Lisa's birthday.

The reason I knew this is that an otherwise-normal-looking gray-haired lady at Portland International Airport used her cell phone to call Lisa and—in the middle of roughly one hundred and fifty people crowded around a gate waiting for a delayed flight—sing *Happy Birthday to You* to her at the top of her lungs.

After the obnoxious musical call, the lady dialed through her address book like a woman possessed, leaving lengthy, loud, personal messages for friends and family members. It was remarkable in a sad sort of way.

She's far from unique. Abusing cell phones is an epidemic. In April 2003, the New York City Council passed a law against using cell phones at the theater and in museums. If you can't control yourself or your phone, you get to pay fifty bucks. In October 2003 in Massachusetts, a man was charged with assault after he allegedly stabbed a person who asked him to turn off his ringing cell phone in a movie theater. And at a 2004 technology conference, one panelist answered his cell phone . . . during his presentation.

I sometimes think people with bad cell phone manners follow me around. In mid-May in San Jose, I sat next to Kevin who wanted his colleague to call Wendy and ensure she "has her shit together for the meeting tomorrow." He spent the next several minutes detailing Wendy's inadequacies. Loudly.

In a bookstore the next day, a sing-song ringtone of "Dixie" startled those of us in the magazine section, but not nearly as much as Linda's conversation with her new boyfriend as they planned dinner at a Mexican restaurant accompanied by a "nightcap" at her nearby apartment.

I spend most of my time teaching executives how to conduct themselves in front of a camera, not how to talk on the phone. But with more than one hundred and twenty million cell phone users in the United States, cell phone abuse is only going to get worse. So in the interest of stemming that rising tide, not to mention preserving my own sanity, here are five tips for polite cell phone etiquette—suitable for passing along to friends, colleagues, and family members.

1. Increase the peace—turn off the ringer at the movies, or theater, or opera. Cell phones come with a vibrate option. Use it. Or turn the damn thing off and pay attention to your son's soccer game.

2. Speak softly—cell phones have very good microphones. There's no need to shout. And, no, you do not have an invisible cloak of secrecy around you in the airport, on the bus, or riding the train. Really.

3. Build barriers—if you're sitting in a public place, you can't have a private conversation. Be considerate of others. Keep a ten-foot barrier between you and the assembled masses.

4. Toilet train—no matter how urgent the need, you don't need to talk while peeing. Yes, I'm talking to you Mr.

Loud Voice in the Denver airport men's room by gate A32 on May 7. One survey indicates that forty-seven percent of adults think it's okay to talk on cell phones while in restrooms. It's not.

5. Watch the road—don't dial while driving—or operating heavy machinery of any kind. To the driver of the tan SUV I saw swerving along I-5 near Seattle in April—this means you. Your child in the back seat will thank you, and so will we.

These are common-sense options; they're just not that common.

If I ruled the world, etiquette violators would receive short, sharp shocks that eventually would elicit a Pavlovian response every time they even thought about using their phone in a public place.

I'm not alone. An industrial design company called Ideo has come up with prototypes of "social" cell phones that deliver a mild electric shock to the user depending on how loud they are—the louder the conversation, the stronger the electric shock.

Talk about an idea whose time has come. If the lady at Portland International Airport had such a phone, she'd still be in the fetal position by gate A2—and deservedly so.

To Lisa—happy birthday. I hope your friend just sends you a card next time.

To Wendy—I hope the meeting went well. Free advice: never tell Kevin anything that you don't want mindlessly broadcast to strangers.

And to Linda's boyfriend—I hope you enjoyed your burrito, but mostly I hope Linda's cell phone stayed silent in her purse before, during, and even after the nightcap.

6
Jumping Fleas and the Power of Analogy

June 2005

Analogies are woefully underused in corporate America. We're all afraid that they're somehow too simplistic; that because we're now grown-ups we should neglect one of the most powerful tools available to us when telling a great story.

So when it comes to corporate communications, it's like we've all become the most boring teacher in high school when we speak or write. Remember that guy? We all hated his class.

A clear analogy, well thought out and well delivered, will do more to advance understanding (and sales) than a month's worth of soulless writing or presentations full of corporate jargon. Why? Because people are built to give and receive stories—and analogies play a major role in storytelling.

For example, one Austin-based chain that sells golf equipment describes itself as a "multi-channel golf retailer." Now just what the hell is that? Well, the company's strategy is to sell golf equipment and clothes online, via catalogs, and in retail stores. In that respect, they want to do for golf retailing what Barnes & Noble did for selling books. Their CEO is fond of saying, "We're like a candy store for golfers," because they spend an average of forty-five minutes in his stores, an unheard of length in retailing.

I hate "multi-channel golf retailer." I love "candy store for golfers" and "the Barnes & Noble of golf." Realistically, the company needs both descriptors. But I know which one makes more sense to me.

In the mid-1990s, Intel CEO Andy Grove listened to a consultant comparing Intel and U.S. Steel. Apparently, some small steel companies had managed to carve out a profitable business selling rebar—concrete reinforced with steel. It was a business that U.S. Steel simply didn't want—but it made the smaller companies a lot of money.

At that time, Intel was pondering a move into cut-price silicon chips. Soon Grove was using the analogy of "silicon rebar" as a way to describe the strategy, which is an incredibly useful thing when it comes to the uber-complicated business of manufacturing computer chips.

Of course, perfect analogies are tough to come by, and in some cases bad ones can have quite the opposite of their intended effect. For example, CBS newsman Dan Rather is famous for his down-home analogies that often leave viewers scratching their heads. My favorite? "If a frog had side pockets he'd probably wear a handgun."

To truly work, analogies have to make immediate sense— by relating to something that has real meaning for your audience. If a boss is "hell on heels" or "linebacker tough," people understand instantly. Want to know if yours works? Test it out on a few folks and see what they say.

For instance, a few weeks back, in response to a question from a curious ten-year-old about just how high a flea can jump, I said, "If fleas were as big as you, they'd be able to jump right over our house in one leap." She took a moment, nodded, and said, "Cool. Thanks, Dad."

What's the best analogy for your company? Do you have one that works well? If you do, you probably already know its power with audiences. If you don't, you could be missing out on an easy way to reach people—because when it comes to communications, we're really a bunch of grown-up kids who just want to hear a great story.

7
So, What Do You Do?

February 2005

On the morning of the first day, I said what I usually say to CEOs: "So what does your company do?" It's a deliberately vague question but the CEO was confident that he and all twelve members of his executive team would be able to answer it—and be relentlessly on-message for external audiences like prospects, customers, partners, and the press.

He was wrong.

I videotaped thirteen different answers. Sure, there were some common elements, but it was clear that the fabric of the answer was stitched together in a pretty haphazard way. The next day I played back seven minutes of footage showing all thirteen executives describing what their company does. It wasn't pretty. After that, I showed them how their competitors were describing themselves. And then I showed them a draft of what I thought they should be saying.

There was a brief, pregnant silence in the room.

"That's it. You nailed it," said one of the company founders.

We talked about nuances and details, but it was clear the company's elevator speech needed to be far more conversational, a lot shorter, a lot more consistent, and much more of a narrative. We needed to lose the jargon, the platitudes, and the "leading provider" syndrome. And we did.

Afterward the CEO of this mid-stage software company buttonholed me in the hall. "You know, if you hadn't shown us how we looked on video, I never would have believed you." I smiled.

"That's why we did," I said.

There are hundreds of companies, big and small, who can't clearly articulate what they do and why anyone should care. It makes me nuts (and I'm not the only one—here's one

reporter's take on the matter: www.pittsburghlive.com/x/
tribune-review/business/s_294201.html.) Even if the CEO
has a good corporate elevator speech, other executives often
don't, which leads to inconsistencies in the answer to that
simplest of questions.

"So, what does your company do?"

8
YouTube-ification of Corporate Communications

January 2007

To cut through the noise and the boring blah of their media machines, some companies are turning to on-line video, spurred in part by the phenomenal success of YouTube, which has become a daily addiction for millions of people.

So instead of the typical e-mail or memo from the boss, you might instead get a short video of the boss talking about the big merger, the big event, the year ahead, or the big award. And that's good—because people like to watch.

Major companies from Monsanto and Wal-Mart to Sun Microsystems and General Motors are using video to talk to shareholders, employees, salespeople, and the general public—without a filter. Traffic to Sun's online pressroom jumped threefold—to around forty-two thousand visitors a month—after it remade the pressroom to incorporate video, according to a January 2, 2007, *Wall Street Journal* article.

Turns out that anyone with a digital video camera and a bit of tech savvy can shoot, edit, and post online short video clips. The question then becomes how to do it well. If you spend five minutes on YouTube, you quickly find out there's a lot of blah up there, along with some super nuggets (and, alas, a lot of Britney Spears sans underwear and people with too much time on their hands making fountains out of Diet Coke and Mentos).

You'll also notice that the most popular videos are typically less than three minutes in length. Just as people spend an average of seven to twelve seconds looking at an individual Web page, they won't tolerate a twenty-five-minute video that's full of jargon and corporate BS.

If you're going to jump into the online video world, there are a few guidelines to follow:

Keep it short—what this means practically is that you get to make one, maybe two, key points. More than that and your video will run too long and probably won't get watched. Anyone can talk for an hour—what would you say if you had three minutes?

Make it compelling—if your CEO could bore for America, get him/her trained ahead of time. Even TV news anchors periodically submit themselves to professional coaching. And lose the corporate-speak. Talk in plain, conversational language. Oh, and have something to say.

Keep it simple—along with a good message and great delivery; keep the music, special effects, and fancy transitions to a minimum. This isn't a rock video; so unless technical razzle-dazzle helps deliver the message, leave it to MTV and ESPN.

Make it relevant—a message that's authentic and timely but only seventy-percent polished is better than a message that's one-hundred-percent polished but two weeks old. The message doesn't need to be fancy, just clear and concise. For example, when Republican U.S. Senator Gordon Smith expressed his frustration with the Iraq War by saying simply, and with great emphasis, "I, for one, am at the end of my rope when it comes to supporting a policy that has our soldiers patrolling the same streets in the same way, being blown up by the same bombs day after day. That is absurd. It may even be criminal. I cannot support that any more."

Respect your audience—when you have a captive audience, often full of subordinates, it's tempting to turn on the verbal fire hose and talk forever. Don't do it. Respect their time and attention span—then give them a URL or e-mail address so they can follow up and continue the conversation as appropriate.

Be creative—not in a CEO-juggles-while-talking-about-earnings way but in a clear way that matches the message. Some of the most popular online videos execute a simple approach well, like OK Go's now-famous "Here It Goes Again" music video clip on YouTube where the group's members spend three minutes stepping on and off four treadmills.

The absolute worst thing you can do is leap eagerly into the online video world and just visually replicate a bad print brochure or inane slide presentation. Like most things, online video takes a bit of time and thought to do well. The good news is that it's not complicated. In fact, the interns at your company are probably already busy posting their own clips and sending them to friends on their own time (or maybe even during office hours).

The YouTube-ification of communications has arrived. So dip a toe into the online video waters. Done well, it can enhance your communications and ultimately your brand. Done badly, well, let's just say you don't want to end up on YouTube as an example of what not to do (like poor Britney).

9
Sucky Writing

March 2005

Does your writing suck? It might, because in corporate America a lot of writing sucks.

There was a time when bad writing just manifested itself in the occasional memo or letter. But that was before e-mail and instant messaging. Of course, you might think bad writing isn't really a big problem for corporations.

You'd be wrong.

Here's one example received by R. Craig Hogan who runs an online business writing school. This is the verbatim text:

"i am writing a essay on writing i work for this company and my boss want me to help improve the workers writing skills can yall help me with some information thank you"

Punctuation, capitalization, grammar, oh my! Where to start? And it's not just this writer. A study of one hundred and twenty companies conducted by the National Commission on Writing found that one-third of employees at blue-chip corporations write poorly—and that the companies were spending up to $3.1 billion annually on remedial training, according to a December 2004 *New York Times* article.

"E-mail is a party to which English teachers have not been invited," Hogan says. "It has companies tearing their hair out."

Even when grammar, capitalization, and punctuation are passable, the writing can still be hysterical. Here's another verbatim note forwarded to Dilbert creator Scott Adams:

"This change will allow us to better leverage our talent base in an area where developmental roles are under way and strategically focuses us toward the upcoming Business System transition where Systems literacy and accuracy will be essential to maintain and to further improve service levels to our customer base going forward."

Now just what the hell does that mean?

The truth is that plain English is always better than jargon—and plain English plus good grammar, spelling, and punctuation is better still. A lot of writing problems come down to poor structure—especially in e-mail messages. Here's a suggested skeleton for e-mail:

1. Grab—Get your audience's attention immediately. Imagine they have ten seconds; chances are they have far less.

2. Explain—What are you telling them? Be clear. Be concise. Be direct. Be specific.

3. Close—If you have a clear result in mind, tell them. What do you want them to do?

It isn't complicated. But it is remarkably rare. Another rarity is writers who take the time to scrub through their copy. Does it have a clear point? Are all the words absolutely necessary? Would it be better to just pick up the phone and call the recipient—or walk down to her office?

Also, E-MAIL WRITTEN IN ALL CAPS IS A NO-NO, UNLESS YOU REALLY DO MEAN TO SHOUT. Figure that you get one word in ALL CAPS per day. Use it judiciously.

Finally, no exclamation points—ever. Really. "People think that throwing multiple exclamation points into a business letter will make their point forcefully," Linda Landis Andrews, who teaches at the University of Illinois told the *New York Times*. "I tell them they're allowed two exclamation points in their whole life."

That's a good model to follow. Good writing isn't out of reach for most people—and it's worth adhering to a series of simple steps to make sure you get your point across.

Otherwise your writing could suck.

10
Press Release Me

February 2003

I hate press releases. I hate the sloppy writing and silly jargon, and I definitely hate the "death by press release" syndrome from which many companies suffer. You know the type—an announcement every Tuesday whether it's news or not.

It makes me crazy.

Try this. Go back and look at your company's press releases for the past few months. Take the opening paragraph of each release, put them all into one e-mail, and then have your mom, spouse, or friend read the e-mail. If that ad hoc test group can't discern from the first paragraph why the release matters, it probably doesn't.

So why does corporate America pump out a total of fifteen hundred press releases a day when most of them get trashed immediately by busy reporters? Well, one reason is that a well-written press release can be a powerful tactical manifestation of a PR strategy. For example, on Monday, March 25, 2002, *Playboy* sent out a one-hundred-and-eighty-two-word press release. Here's the opening sentence:

"Enron's female employees whose working days have hit a snag are about to get a second chance. *Playboy* magazine is conducting a search for the "Women of Enron" to pose in one of its upcoming issues."

The media coverage was enormous; the tie-in to current events surrounding Enron was compelling, and the wave of publicity continued until the August 2002 issue of *Playboy* hit newsstands.

Compare that to another March announcement, by Microsoft—usually no slouch in the PR department—about its new facility in Silicon Valley. Here's the ninety-seven-word opening paragraph from that eight-hundred-and-sixty-word press release:

"Microsoft Corp. (Nasdaq: MSFT) Chairman and Chief Software Architect Bill Gates today announced the official opening of the new Microsoft Technology Center-Silicon Valley (MTC-SV) in Mountain View, Calif. Aimed at empowering valley-based businesses with an interactive environment, innovative technology concepts and dedicated consulting support, the MTC-SV will expand Microsoft's investment in the valley and bring an environment of collaboration and growth where customers can learn how to take advantage of the scalability, flexibility and manageability of the Microsoft®.NET Enterprise Servers, and use Visual Studio®.NET to develop Web services for the Microsoft®.NET Framework."

Now it's horribly unfair to compare pictures of naked women to Bill Gates, although each is appealing in its own way, I suppose. And while Microsoft opening a facility in an area where it is widely despised is newsworthy, you certainly wouldn't know it from the release, which is unimaginative, wordy, and downright dull.

What if Microsoft focused on a stunt? "Microsoft will open a technology center in Silicon Valley today and eat humble pie. Literally. It's the featured dessert at the launch event."

What if it highlighted its whip-smart people? "Nav Bhachech can't sit still. He's the lead consultant for Microsoft's Technology Center in Silicon Valley. He commands 26,000 square feet of space, 10 computer laboratories, and the respect of his colleagues for focusing on a tech community that's crucial to Microsoft's future."

There's a happy medium between dry corporate language and punchy newspaper copy—and that's where press releases should live. There are ways to market even lesser events using press releases, but it takes some thought and a strategic approach. Here are five suggestions for press-release success:

5. Brevity—more than six hundred words is unnecessary. If you can't say it concisely, it won't work. And brevity mixed with creativity is cookies and cream.

4. Clarity—say it in plain language. If people don't understand your news, they won't act. If you fill your release with jargon and nonsense, they won't understand *or* act. Plain English works best.

3. Selectiveness—don't spam the world with announcements. It will mask those times when you really do have news.

2. Strategy—make a press release part of an overall media-relations strategy. A lone press release is like a lone rifleman—it's far better to have riflemen backed up by machine gunners, artillery, and air power.

1. **News**—news releases should contain news. Your company developing a cancer breakthrough is news. Your company moving to new office space is not news.

Press releases have become a permanent part of corporate America. They're often mandatory for publicly traded companies. But that doesn't mean the world needs to know that your assistant vice president has been promoted to vice president. It doesn't relieve you from having a PR strategy before putting pen to paper. And it certainly doesn't mean you have to write dull copy that puts readers to sleep.

I hate that.

11
Getting Elected by Getting Real

September 2007

Here's what I like the most about forty-five-year-old Democratic presidential candidate Barack Obama: when it comes to communications, he's the anti-Gore. That's a compliment.

When he ran for president in 2000, Al Gore was so stiff when speaking, he could have been stuffed. He didn't seem real, and as GOP communications guru Frank Luntz told one reporter, "'Real' is in for 2008."

And, hopefully, 'real' is in permanently.

Obama's been real for some time. Think back to his

passionate speech at the 2004 Democratic National Convention. His delivery was emotive and almost evangelical; he weaved a series of stories—most notably his own—into a narrative that electrified the crowd and lifted this self-proclaimed "skinny kid with a funny name" to national prominence. In one speech. In just twenty minutes.

Obama is a new voice, but he isn't naive when it comes to the political jujitsu of framing issues and smoothly delivering talking points. For example, if you dissect his August 22, 2007, appearance on *The Daily Show* you can easily see his stock response to the issue of his relative inexperience, something his political opponents often raise. His two talking points in response to that question are:

1. Nobody had more experience than Dick Cheney and Donald Rumsfeld.

2. What people really want is good judgment.

But the real magic of Obama is that when he delivers those message points, he sounds totally conversational and completely compelling. If you look at this ninety-second clip on YouTube, you'll see what I mean. http://www.youtube.com/watch?v=TrSOekKHacA

Notice how Obama subtly reframes the question by saying, "When people talk about experience, what they really want to know is 'Does he have good judgment?'" Then he continues in an extremely engaging manner, controlling the interview.

By contrast, Gore (or John Kerry) would probably have launched into a lengthy dissertation on the value of experience and a laundry list of parliamentary votes he cast to illustrate his experience and political resume. And three minutes in, everyone would have been asleep. Obama not only knows what to say, he knows how to say it, and he knows to get there quickly—and that's quite different.

Running for president is a complicated endeavor. However, if Obama wins the Democratic nomination or even the general election, effective communications will be a big reason why. In fact, Obama's communications skills should put a lot of the more wooden presidential candidates on notice. Gore isn't running this time. But, as communicators, rival Democratic candidates Hillary Clinton and John Edwards aren't in Obama's league.

It's a long time until November 4, 2008, but if Obama keeps his message simple, keeps delivering it well, and keeps away from the gaffes that can derail any campaign, we could have someone in the Oval Office who actually talks like a human being—a refreshing thought in many ways.

12
One Last HPS for the Gipper

August 2004

On October 21, 1984, President Ronald Reagan and fifty-six-year-old Democratic challenger Walter Mondale debated at the Municipal Auditorium in Kansas City, Missouri.

At seventy-three, Reagan was already the oldest president in U.S. history—too old, whispered some Democrats. But Reagan defused the issue in two quick sentences, telling a watching nation, "I want you to know that also I will not make age an issue of this campaign. I am not going to exploit, for political purposes, my opponent's youth and inexperience."

Even Mondale had to smile. It was a masterstroke. One memorable quote among many from a two-term president who came to be known as the "Great Communicator."

Love him or loathe him, Reagan was a fabulous speaker. But more than that, he understood staging—and it changed the presidency forever.

After he defeated President Jimmy Carter in 1980, Reagan installed a cast of stage managers who meticulously thought through each and every public appearance. They even developed their own acronym, "HPS," for headline, picture, story. Every time Reagan appeared in public, the team carefully planned what story with what headline and—most importantly—what picture would accompany the president's message.

Back in the 1980s when ketchup was a vegetable, this was a new approach, and its effectiveness was remarkable. Reagan, the former actor, reveled in the theater of the presidency. His former chief of staff Ken Duberstein said, "People used to say, 'How can an actor be president?' And Reagan's answer was, 'How can somebody be president without being an actor?'"

HPS is not without risks—the media hate staged, pseudo-news events, but as the stage managers knew, eyes almost always beat ears in terms of what citizens remember. Also, HPS works only if there is a modicum of truth in what's being communicated. That's something for all politicians and corporate executives to remember.

It's been awhile since Reagan's state funeral and interment. What do you remember? Was it the riderless horse with the boots facing backward? Was it the pomp and circumstance in DC's National Cathedral? Was it the meticulously timed sunset burial at Reagan's Simi Valley library?

There were any number of touching moments during the ceremonies—but they happened not by chance, but by staging. For example, the original plan for the interment was to have cameras facing the Reagan memorial and a cluster of oak trees. However, that wasn't a good enough visual to support the desired message (in case you missed it: *the Gipper takes the final few steps on his journey into the sunset of his life—remembered as the leader who faced down Communism*). The team rotated the camera angles by ninety degrees so the backdrop was mountains and—most metaphorically—the setting sun.

It was a beautiful, poignant moment. And it was completely custom-made for television.

So did that matter? Did the American public feel

deceived by the staging supporting the outpouring that one wag coined "Gipper porn"? No, because there was truth and genuine feeling attached. Frank Rich wrote in the June 13, 2004, *New York Times*, "As any professional actor can tell you, no performance, however sonorous, can be credible if it doesn't contain at least a kernel of emotional truth."

Scorn for staging rains down when the truth is lacking. Remember Michael Dukakis tooling around in a tank trying to look tough but only succeeding in looking like a dork? Or George W. Bush's flight-deck landing and premature "Mission Accomplished" banner?

Done well, HPS can help elevate a story or a message. It can exemplify the very best of a person or an organization. Done badly, HPS is a tool for crass liars. And it can shield a sham—but only for a limited time.

The truth about Reagan will emerge as the partisan darts and laurels fade, and the historians take over. But for now his team's last HPS work effectively nudged our collective memories of what was good about Reagan, his humor, grace, and leadership while blurring our focus on his significant blind spots—a fondness for budget deficits and a benign neglect of Americans who were poor, nonwhite, or gay.

The Great Communicator was a practiced, polished speaker—something sadly lacking among many politicians and corporate executives. But his real edge was that he understood staging.

Corporations should, too. But they should be careful with their HPS efforts—because the line between the maudlin and the magnificent is awfully thin and even accomplished communications pros don't always know where it is.

13
Red Light, Green Light,
Keep Tight

October 2004

In this bitterly divided election season we can all agree on one thing about Democratic presidential hopeful John Kerry: he doesn't know when to shut up.

Saturday Night Live captured this tendency perfectly in a show that aired during the presidential debates when a comedian playing Kerry said, "I should just sit down, confident in the fact that I just cleaned the president's clock, and not say anything else. But I'm not going to do that. No, I'm gonna keep on talking. Why? Because I can't help myself."

The real debates featured forced brevity in two-minute chunks. Kerry and President Bush were each governed by a traffic-light-type device that shone green, yellow, or red depending on how much time they had left. There was also a buzzer system in case they ran over their allotted time. They didn't.

I think Kerry should carry one of those devices with him for the rest of his life, because forced brevity helped him—just like it could help every senior executive in corporate America.

We've all had the experience of listening to a politician or an executive who can't shut up—and frequently doesn't have to because he outranks everyone else in the room. It's frustrating because human beings typically have short attention spans. That doesn't mean they're inattentive idiots. It just means they're busy and they want speakers to get to the point.

The public speaking group Toastmasters also uses a system of lights in its meetings to indicate when a speaker's time is up. In Toastmasters speaking competitions, anyone who goes over time is automatically disqualified. Wouldn't that be great in the political and corporate worlds?

Of course, it takes a long time to deliver a short speech

well. As one famous speaker once said, "If you want me to deliver a two-hour speech I'm ready right now. If you want a ten-minute speech I'll need two weeks to prepare."

Brevity comes from practice. If speakers have two hours, they typically fill the time. If speakers use Microsoft Power-Point, they typically spend more time preparing the slides than practicing their delivery—which is a huge mistake. For every hour of rehearsal before a speech, each speaker probably increases positive audience perception by ten percent. And isn't that the point—to communicate effectively—quality versus quantity?

I have a fantasy. In it, I'm asked to give the commencement address at a prestigious university. It's an unbearably hot day and the graduating students are in heavy gowns and mortarboards. As I walk up to the podium, I pull out an egg timer. I tell the students my speech will be precisely ten minutes long and I set the egg timer to nine minutes and thirty seconds. Toward the end of my speech the timer goes off; I immediately say "in conclusion," finish up my speech, and get a standing ovation.

Then I wake up and remember I was sitting on my couch watching John Kerry talk when I fell asleep.

14
Can You See What
I'm Saying?

January 2004

President Bush didn't like the questions—and it showed. In an interview with ABC's Diane Sawyer broadcast December 16, 2003, Bush—like many chief executives—displayed a range of nonverbal tics that muddied the message he wanted to communicate.

In the interview, Sawyer quickly homed in on the issue of whether Iraq had "weapons of mass destruction" before American troops invaded last March. As he listened to the questions Bush fidgeted; he blinked rapidly, sucked on his lower lip, and sighed. His eyes darted around and his chin jutted out. At times he was visibly frustrated with Sawyer's line of questioning. In short, he sent a clear signal that was far louder than his words.

He just flat out didn't want to be there.

Bush isn't alone. We all have tics or habits that betray our true feelings. Being on television applies a magnifying glass to them.

And that's a problem, because up to ninety percent of all communication is nonverbal. A classic 1971 study by UCLA psychologist Albert Mehrabian showed that when asked what they remembered about a speaker from a verbal, vocal, and visual standpoint, audience members indicated just seven percent of their recall was verbal (what was said), but thirty-eight percent of their recall was vocal (how it was said) and fifty-five percent was visual (the speaker's body language and confidence).

This is human cognitive behavior and a lesson for all executives, chief and otherwise. You say far more with your nonverbal expressions than you do with your mouth—so watch them. And while you're watching those nonverbal behaviors beware of another message-deflating tic, the verbal accompaniment to fidgeting: um disease.

Here's a cure for um disease (if job security isn't an issue): click your fingers every time your boss says "um" and see what happens. If you're still on the premises, chances are those ums will dry up almost instantly. Toastmasters has a novel approach in this area: every time a speaker uses a nonword like "um," "ah," or "er," a marble is dropped into a can. It's a Pavlovian method. But it works.

Another psychologist, Frieda Goldman-Eisler, found that up to fifty percent of speech is actually silence. She reckoned speakers used nonwords while they were thinking of what to say next—which is fine at Rotary, but less comforting when it's the leader of a publicly held company, your boss, or the leader of the free world.

Chief executives have to talk to the media—it's part of their gig. And reporters can ask tough questions that trip those CEOs—it's part of their gig. But more often executives trip themselves, betraying stated messages by exhibiting bad nonverbal skills, suffering from um disease, and having the arrogance to think they can just wing it in interviews or speeches.

Communicating a clear message and answering questions posed by reporters is a delicate dance. Like most things, it takes practice to do well. And the best practice for media interviews is videotaped coaching—something CEOs often view beforehand with about as much fondness as a root canal, but afterward wonder how they lived without.

Executives who don't submit to videotaped coaching before media interviews are fooling themselves and flying without a safety net. If a chief executive hasn't practiced concise answers to the top ten rude questions he will be asked, then he's a fool. If she doesn't know to pause long enough to formulate a good answer, she's not helping her organization. And if he doesn't want to be there, no amount of words will overcome the nonverbal signals that make up ninety percent of a message.

So whether you're a CEO, an executive, or a product manager who wants to clearly communicate a point, watch your nonverbal communication and vaccinate against um disease by submitting to videotaped coaching before media contact. Your electorate—that is, the reporters, employees, shareholders, and investors who each have a stake in your performance—will thank you for it.

15
You Like Me,
You Really Like Me

March 2004

In 2004 America will select a new president, and two things will likely decide the election.

Knowledge of the issues? Leadership skills? Experience? Position on gay marriage?

No. Likability and height. Sounds crazy, right?

But it's not. Since 1960, the Gallup organization has conducted its "Personality Factor Poll" before every presidential election. The only consistent prognosticator of the final election results: the likability factor. In his book *You've Got to*

Be Believed to be Heard, speech coach Bert Decker writes, "The personality factor dominates in politics. It also dominates in business. And it dominates in our day-to-day lives."

He's right. It's human nature. We want to be liked and we want to like our leaders. Have you ever loved or hated your boss? It's just as well there's no electoral college for CEOs or a lot of them could be in trouble. I once worked for a boss for whom half the staff in our office would have run through a brick wall. I also worked for her successor, a boss who would have needed that brick wall just to protect him from that same staff.

Likability is a real factor in real life. But on videotape it screams. Likable leaders who smile, make eye contact, and convey a genuine respect for other people come across well. Less likable leaders don't. One major-company executive I know had a body coach for a period of time. The coach followed him everywhere and tried to help him soften his aggressive body language. Why? Because employees were scared of him. They didn't like him.

These factors matter. It's simple human emotion, and if it helps get the leader of the free world elected, it's something to which any boss should pay attention. And politics, like the corporate world, is strongly influenced by human emotion.

"They don't teach this in political science, but if a politician is liked, he or she is halfway home." Llewellyn King, publisher of *White House Weekly*, wrote in a recent opinion column. "You can find President Bush's grasp of world affairs risible, his command of English tenuous, and his lack of curiosity appalling, but he is still hard to dislike. He is hugely, damnably, annoyingly likable."

That could present a problem for the presumptive Democratic nominee, sixty-year-old Senator John Kerry, who has the impossibly sad visage of a basset hound. It's not really fair. A politician spends his entire life boning up on foreign policy, fighting for his country, and working in government, only to find voters like the other guy's smile. Remember the smartest kid in your high school class? No one really liked that guy. To be fair, Kerry has worked hard to become more agreeable. He even rode his motorcycle on stage during a Jay Leno visit. But he's still more Al Gore than Bill Clinton.

And here's another predictor of presidential prowess: height.

This sounds just as weird as likability, but according to a December 2003 *Washington Post* story, of the thirteen presidential elections in the television era, ten were won by the taller candidate. The three smaller victors? Nixon in 1972, Carter in 1976, and Bush in 2000. Although Bush at 5'11" hardly qualifies as short, he did edge out the 6'1" Al Gore (see likability: lack of, above).

Bush is the first person under six feet tall to occupy the Oval Office in the last two decades. The Post writer, who obviously has too much time on his hands, also studied thirty-one U.S. Senate elections and found the taller candidate prevailed in twenty-three of the races.

So, long before he self-destructed in the now infamous "I Have a Scream" speech, the 5'9" Howard Dean wasn't going to win the presidency. Not only is he shortish, but he was also described as "emotionally chilly" by at least one writer. And we won't even pick on the 5'7" Dennis Kucinich.

There's nothing fair about either of these presidential predictors. But they're both meaningful to voters. So put aside those pesky issues of the day. What matters is likability and height. It's silly, but apparently serious enough to make a real difference.

If we could draw up a perfect president from central casting, he (and chances are it'll be a "he" at least until 2008) would be tall, friendly, and extremely likable. Oh, a working knowledge of the government and world affairs would be nice, too. But it's not essential. Such are the human vagaries that elect the leader of the free world—and affect our opinions of business leaders across the corporate world.